THE FORGOTTEN CANALS OF YORKSHIRE
WAKEFIELD TO SWINTON VIA BARNSLEY

The Barnsley and Dearne & Dove Canals

TRANSPORT THROUGH THE AGES

Transport Through the Ages is a new and fascinating collection of transport titles, brought to you by Wharncliffe Books. This delightful series is intended to highlight the various modes of transport from the canal to the railway age, exploring the transitional journey of their operation. These highly illustrated books, contain astounding pictures, spanning the last century, which captivate the history and nostalgia of the locality.

OTHER TITLES IN THE SERIES:

Canals & River Sections of the Aire & Calder Navigation
Mike Taylor
ISBN: 1-903425-37-9
£9.99

Trams Around Dewsbury & Wakefield
Norman Ellis
ISBN: 1-903425-40-9
£9.99

Trams & Trolleybuses in Doncaster
Richard Buckley
ISBN: 1-903425-29-8
£9.99

OTHER LOCAL TITLES:

Esk Valley Railways
Alan Whitworth
ISBN: 1-903425-49-5
£5.99

Walkers, Writers & Watering Holes
Barrie Pepper & Jack Thompson
ISBN: 1-871647-86-X
£9.95

Barnsley Buses
Stephen Farnsworth & Roger Glister
ISBN: 1-871647-91-6
£9.99

The Making of the West Yorkshire Landscape
Anthony Silson
ISBN: 1-903425-31-X
£9.99

Please contact us via any of the methods below for more information or a catalogue.
WHARNCLIFFE BOOKS
47 Church Street – Barnsley – South Yorkshire – S70 2AS
Tel: 01226 734555 – 734222 Fax: 01226 724438
E-mail: enquiries@pen-and-sword.co.uk – Website www.wharncliffebooks.co.uk

THE FORGOTTEN CANALS OF YORKSHIRE

Wakefield to Swinton via Barnsley
The Barnsley and Dearne & Dove Canals

Roger Glister

Series Editor
Brian Elliott

Wharncliffe Books

In memory of Alan Hall

First published in Great Britain in 2004
and reprinted in 2011 and 2016 by
WHARNCLIFFE BOOKS
An imprint of
Pen & Sword Books Ltd
47 Church Street
Barnsley, South Yorkshire
S70 2AS

ISBN 978 1 90342 538 1

A CIP catalogue record for this book is
available from the British Library

Printed and bound in England
By 4edge Limited

Pen & Sword Books Ltd incorporates the Imprints of Aviation, Atlas,
Family History, Fiction, Maritime, Military, Discovery, Politics, History,
Archaeology, Select, Wharncliffe Local History, Wharncliffe True Crime,
Military Classics, Wharncliffe Transport, Leo Cooper, The Praetorian Press,
Remember When, Seaforth Publishing and Frontline Publishing.

For a complete list of Pen & Sword titles please contact
PEN & SWORD BOOKS LIMITED
47 Church Street, Barnsley, South Yorkshire, S70 2AS, England
E-mail: enquiries@pen-and-sword.co.uk
Website: www.pen-and-sword.co.uk

CONTENTS

CHAPTER ONE

The Barnsley Canal

Introduction

In July 1792 the Aire & Calder Navigation Company instructed its manager, William Martin, to obtain a plan and estimate for the building of a canal from Barnsley to Wakefield. This scheme was to facilitate the exploitation of the vast coal reserves beneath the environs of these two towns. Thus on 7 August the Aire & Calder Navigation shareholders' meeting asked William Jessop, the company's consulting engineer, to survey a route to be presented at a public meeting. Jessop at this time was heavily committed to other canal projects and was too busy to survey either the Barnsley Canal or the Dearne & Dove Canal that had also been offered to him. Subsequently the job fell to William Martin and his assistants, John Gott and Elias Wright, who promptly surveyed several routes between the Aire & Calder and Barnsley.

They do not appear to have wasted a lot of time, for, on 20 September the shareholders were told by Jessop that he had perused the various routes surveyed and in his opinion one line in particular, from Wakefield to Barnsley, with a branch to Silkstone, 'Will be Practicable, be a very eligible Line to be Adopted and that the Expense upon a cursory View wou'd not exceed the Sum of Fifty Thousand Pounds'.

A public subscription meeting was held at the *White Bear Hotel* in Barnsley, now the *Royal Hotel*, on 15 October 1792 with a leading Aire & Calder Navigation proprietor, John Smyth of Heath, in the chair. The route and estimate, now revised to £60,000, was presented to those in attendance and no fewer than eighty-six investors quickly subscribed the capital sum.

The principal shareholder, who invested £1,600, was Walter Spencer-Stanhope of Cannon Hall. He stood to gain vast sums with the building of the Barnsley Canal due to his ownership of the land around Silkstone beneath which lay the rich Silkstone coal seams.

Born plain Walter Stanhope in 1749, the son of a Leeds cloth merchant, he added Spencer to his name upon succession to the Cannon Hall estates from his uncle, ironmaster John Spencer. Already a trustee of the A & C N due to stock he gained by his marriage in 1738, he was made chairman of the Barnsley Canal Company, a position he enjoyed throughout the building of the waterway. There can be little doubt that it was he who lobbied for the five tramroads linking points on the coalfield with the canal at Barnby that were included in the Parliamentary Bill that was now prepared.

The Barnsley Canal duly received its Royal assent on 3 June 1793, at a cost of £2,000 to the promoters, with confirmed capital of £80,000 to cover the latest estimate of £72,000. On the same day the Dearne & Dove Bill was also given assent.

The first sod was cut on Heath Common by William Martin, who had been

A loaded coal barge exits the Barnsley Canal onto the Calder & Hebble Navigation and turns toward Castleford and Goole. This picture, taken in the late 1800s shows the toll house on the right and the lock-keeper closing the head gate to prepare the lock for the next boat. The small but wide rowing boats in the foreground were probably for hire.

Lock number 1 again with clinker-built barges tied up awaiting orders. This, and the previous picture, show this lock in its final position, close to the river, having been relocated in 1816.

appointed company treasurer, on 27 September 1793. The contractor was John Pinkerton, well known for his work on a number of canals and closely associated with William Jessop. Pinkerton's weakness was a well developed ability to miscalculate estimates which resulted in skimped works and disputes with his employers. The Barnsley commission was to be no different and Samuel Hartley, the company surveyor, was soon at odds with the contractor.

By the summer of 1794 Pinkerton was experiencing great difficulty in the Cold Hiendley cutting and needed large amounts of gunpowder for blasting that had not been anticipated which meant very slow progress being made in this area. The making of the whole line, excluding locks, had been expected to cost about 6d (2.5p) per yard in the main and no-where more than 1s 4d (6.66p). However, no less than 5,000 yards had cost almost 2s (10p) and one stretch at Cold Hiendley over 4s (20p) per yard, therefore vastly over budget.

Despite the bickerings, specification changes and construction setbacks, the majority of the earthworks were completed by the middle of 1793 and Hartley was able to report that the canal was in water from the top of the Walton flight of locks to Barnsley. He also had to report that the top five locks on the flight may have to be demolished and rebuilt due to the puddle not being carried under the foundations correctly.

The completion of the works resulted in the opening of the Barnsley Canal on 8 June 1799, from the Aire & Calder at Heath to Barnsley Basin. The remaining length to the terminus at Barnby Basin was finally opened in early 1802. The total expenditure by the company from the canal's inception to its completion was £95,000. The litigation between the Canal Company and John Pinkerton was not resolved until 1812 when the contractor paid £3,137 to the Company in compensation for unfinished and remedial work.

The waterway was sixteen miles in length with a navigable depth of five feet. There were fifteen locks between the Calder and the summit level with three at Agbrigg and twelve at Walton which were built originally to accommodate craft of 58 feet long by 14 feet 10 inches in width. These were increased in size to 79 feet by 14 feet 10 inches wide in 1881 and the depth of the channel increased to six feet. The water supply was taken from a reservoir built at Cold Hiendley which was inadequate from the start. Enlarged in 1839, the reservoir still proved too small and another, Wintersett, was constructed in 1854 adjacent to the first. There was insufficient capacity even then and a final attempt was made to alleviate the problem in 1874 when the total area of the reservoirs was increased to 55 acres.

Knowing that an adequate supply of water would be crucial to the smooth running of the canal, William Jessop designed the lock chambers of each flight to have equal falls: eight feet on the Barnby flight and seven feet six inches on the Agbrigg/Walton flight. This, coupled with identical dimensions, ensured that when one lock emptied, its contents would exactly fill the chamber below with out wasting any water. This feature also meant that lock gates were interchangeable.

The Dearne & Dove Canal and the Don Navigation were protected by a stipulation in the Barnsley Bill calling for a stop-lock at the junction of the two canals. This lock, situated at Hoyle Mill, prevented loss of water in both directions and was jointly managed. The Barnsley Company was also

Number 1 lock with an empty barge being horse-drawn into the first pound of the Barnsley Canal. More pleasure boats can be seen to the right.

Just over a mile from the junction, the Heath to Walton road crosses the canal by Heath Bridge. It was also known as 'The Lover's Bridge'; though records do not say how this name was earned, the secluded and tranquil situation may have had a lot to do with it!

Heath Bridge,
Near Wakefield.

forbidden to extract any water from the River Dearne.

The most handsome structure on the waterway was the aqueduct over the River Dearne at Hoyle Mill. Originally an embankment with one thirty foot arch for the river had been envisaged but the Woolley Edge Rock was found to outcrop on both sides of the valley and Jessop decided to construct a masonry aqueduct of five thirty foot arches. This monument to the canal builder's art cost £1,547 and was used as the company logo on toll tickets and other paperwork.

In 1799 the first lock at Agbrigg was located at the end of a long cutting some way from the River Calder. This proved troublesome as when the river level rose in times of flood the cut became choked with debris and the entrance tended to silt up. In 1816 this was remedied by making a new cut slightly to the west and moving the lock closer to the river.

The other locks on the canal were a flight of five that lifted the canal to its terminus at Barnby. The water for these locks was obtained by back pumping up the flight and using the same water again. This was done using a steam powered beam engine pump built by the Low Moor Iron Company at a cost of £1,630. The coalfield at Barnby Furnace, operated by the Low Moor Company, was now able to develop and the product made up fifty percent of the coal carried down the waterway to the Calder. Manufactured goods were also carried away from Barnsley while a good return trade was soon established transporting building materials, agricultural produce and limestone. The latter was brought up the canal from Brotherton and Knottingley in large quantities to be burnt in kilns built at Barnby Basin and Barugh.

Despite the authority to build the essential tramroads from the Silkstone collieries being incorporated in the Act of Parliament granted to construct the canal, only the Low Moor Company had so far taken advantage of the clause with a half mile long tramway from the colliery at Barnby Furnace to the canal head. By 1804 its output had reached 10,000 tons but due to geological faults the mine was closed by the end of 1806. At the time only one other colliery was producing coal in any quantity. This was the Silkstone Colliery, operated by Samuel Thorp of Banks Hall, which had very precarious transport links with the canal along a roadway that was quite impassable in wet weather. During 1807 it was quite usual to find between five and ten boats waiting for loads and be idle for anything up to a week at a time.

This sorry state of affairs soon began to tell on the company's finances and the situation deteriorated to the point where the treasurer reported debts amounting to about £44,000 with less than £10 in hand to meet them. Desperate measures were needed, and at a special shareholders' meeting in October 1807 the Company sought approval to raise the £43,000 required to satisfy the main creditors and build the tramways to serve the working collieries in the Silkstone coalfield.

During 1808 the lines were surveyed, land was purchased and construction put in hand. Some of the land belonged to Walter Spencer-Stanhope, the principal shareholder and chairman of the Barnsley Canal Company and who, despite the Company's difficulties, had no qualms about charging £100 an acre for it. The resultant tramway was built to a gauge of four feet two inches using cast iron double flanged rail spiked to stone sleeper blocks laid diagonally

A loaded barge and its crew pose for a photograph whilst the horse stands waiting patiently, grateful for the rest.

Lock number 11 looking towards Wakefield with Soap House Bridge that carries the B6376 Walton to Crofton road over the canal. The following three photographs were taken in 1953.

to the line. It ran for two miles from Barnby Basin to Silkstone Bridge and was fully operational by mid-1810. The three foot long rail sections came mainly from the Low Moor Company's foundry but some were obtained from Isaac Aydon's foundry at Wakefield. At the time of opening two concerns were making use of the new railway: Samuel Thorp and Jonas Clarke. The former had made preparations for the arrival of the railway by the construction of a short branch line to his already operational pits at Banks Hall. Jonas Clarke, however, had awaited the coming of the railway before developing his colliery at the south end of the village of Silkstone.

Their monopoly was short lived due to the arrival of Thomas and Daniel Wilson who re-opened the colliery at Barnby Furnace and developed pits to the east of the line. Another short branch to Norcroft Bridge was constructed by Richard Stringer and Joseph Popplewell, with rails provided by John Darwin & Co at Elsecar Ironworks, to serve another new colliery. These four coal companies provided the bulk of the trade for the Barnsley Canal for the next ten years. Nearly half of the product from the Silkstone coalfield only used the Barnsley Canal as far as the junction with the Dearne & Dove where it proceeded to the Dun Navigation at Swinton and thence to Lincolnshire. The rest travelled the full length of the Barnsley Canal and made its way to the Ouse via the Aire & Calder Navigation. A not inconsiderable tonnage of coal from the collieries around Worsbrough was also using the Barnsley Canal to reach the markets of the Vale of York and an unusual sight on the upper reaches of the Dearne & Dove Canal would have been laden coal barges passing in both directions.

The development of the Silkstone Railway was the saving of the Barnsley Canal in its early years. From an annual tonnage of coal in 1808 of 34,673 it rose without fail each year to 85,355 in 1813 and, with some slight faltering, to 114,353 in 1820. This was some consolation for the long suffering shareholders who enjoyed a steadily rising dividend; in 1820 the Company paid a princely seven-and-a-half percent.

Throughout the early years both the Barnsley and the Dearne & Dove canals had been plagued by a shortage of water and the first of several steps to alleviate the problem was taken in 1807 when the reservoir at Cold Hiendley was enlarged. In 1854 a second reservoir, Wintersett, was built adjacent to the original and this in turn was increased in size by 55 acres in 1874. At this time a pumping engine was installed at Cold Hiendley to raise the excess water from this into the larger Wintersett reservoir. This beam engine, made at Harvey's of Hale, was still working shortly after the Second World War. Coal for the steam plant was delivered to the site by narrow boats that navigated the feeder that ran from the canal near Haw Park Bridge and was one of only a few roles played by such craft on this broad canal.

In 1828 the Aire & Calder proposed to rebuild the line of the Calder to enable the passage of larger vessels from the Humber to Wakefield and beyond. The Barnsley Canal Company supported this scheme and to this end Joseph Atkinson, the resident engineer appointed in 1823, made an announcement that he would be raising and re-aligning most of the bridges on the canal, 'to enable that Description of Sea-going Vessels called Billy-boys to navigate up the Line.' He was of the opinion that these craft would be capable and willing

Soap House Bridge again, this time showing the lock chamber and its mainly brick construction, though stone copings have been used. This bridge was also known as High Town Bridge.

The B6376 crossing the canal at Soap Houses. It can be seen how these original bridges now form a bottleneck where they cut down the road width to early 1800s standards.

to transport Silkstone coal direct from the West Riding of Yorkshire to coastal ports without trans-shipment. Unfortunately, Mr Atkinson died before his plan was fully implemented and it was his successor, Mr W T Hall, who made the declaration in January 1830 that all the necessary alterations having been made to the bridges, 'all BILLY BOYS, COASTING and other VESSELS of not more than 14 Feet 10 Inches Beam, may now pass along the whole of the Canal for Silkstone Coal, Merchandise, &c.' So reported the *Doncaster Gazette* on 8 January, 1830.

Billy Boys were basically seagoing vessels carrying 80 to 100 tons and built along the same lines as the better known keels. Being of clinker construction with very bluff bows and more pronounced shear, they were about 63 feet long with a beam of some 18 feet and, like the keels, carried leeboards. They were twin-masted with a bowsprit and carried sloop style rigging which was not the most convenient of sailing rigs to dismantle and stow on deck whilst the craft navigated a low bridge on the canal. As the Billy Boys drew considerably more water than a keel and were more than four feet wider it would be reasonable to assume that none took advantage of Mr Hall's extensive alterations to the infrastructure of the Barnsley Canal. They did, however, make occasional visits to Leeds and Wakefield using the upgraded Aire & Calder Navigation.

The first signs of the storm clouds gathering on the horizon came with the proposed North Midland Railway line from Derby to Leeds and the Barnsley Canal Company found itself objecting to the Bill in order to ensure that any bridges over the canal were built to the same dimensions as those on the Goole Canal should they wish at a later date to increase its capacity. This they did in September 1836 by deepening the canal to seven feet by raising the banks and lock walls. The reservoir at Cold Hiendley also had its capacity increased by heightening the embankment. The North Midland opened in 1840 and was quickley followed in 1841 by the Great North of England Railway that ran from Darlington to York and it was this concern that heralded the decline of the Barnsley Canal.

An entry in the Proprietors' Minute Book on 6 July 1842 illustrated the early inroads made by the new railway into the canal trade. It was recorded that this line from Darlington was carrying

> a considerable quantity of Coal into the neighbourhood of Ripon, Boro'bridge, York etc. which was formerly supplied by Mr Clarke's Silkstone Coal to the extent of about Fifty thousand Tons per Annum.

Coal tonnage on the canal continued to fall as more and more cheaper coal from outlying coalfields arrived by rail to satisfy the needs of the Barnsley's former customers. By 1844, the Great North of England Railway had cut its rates to 1/4d per mile with which neither Barnsley Canal or the Aire & Calder Navigation could compete.

After several acrimonious meetings with both the Aire & Calder and the Don Navigation the Barnsley Canal remained independent in a chaotic, cut-throat world of railway expansion where both the old and the new transport systems were fighting for survival. When the Don Navigation took over the Dearne & Dove Canal in January 1846 after long negotiations they cut their tolls by more than fifty per cent, thus damaging the Barnsley even further and

This is lock 14 with its footbridge giving access to Upper Lock House at about three miles from the Calder & Hebble.

This picture shows a laden motor barge passing beneath Walton Hall Bridge that carried the driveway to Walton Hall. In the background is lock 15. From lock 14 to beyond Haw Park Bridge, Squire Waterton of Walton Hall built a twelve foot high wall between his grounds and the canal to discourage poaching by canal boatmen on his estate.

On this photograph the canal is travelling through Walton Cutting. The photographer is standing on Haw Park Bridge. In this picture the canal is in decline with weed and debris in the very shallow channel.

this proved to be the final straw; they began looking for a buyer. A period of horse-trading then commenced between the Manchester and Leeds Railway, the Manchester, Sheffield and Lincolnshire Railway and the Aire & Calder Navigation. The Barnsley Canal Company flirted with each of the bidders in turn but failed to reach an agreement during which time the Company's position was steadily weakening. The tonnage of coal carried by the canal had dropped from 204,000 tons in 1844 to 84,000 in 1853 owing to the amount of trade taking advantage of the cheaper tolls on the Dearne & Dove. As the Barnsley Canal was a source of trade for the Aire & Calder and, like the Don Navigation, it wanted to protect the Silkstone coalfield from total exploitation by the railways a strong representation was made to the Company which, at last recognising the futility of independence, capitulated. A Bill authorising the transfer was introduced in 1856 but the Barnsley Company remained in existence to carry on some of the formal business.

The trade to York was still diminishing in an alarming manner; from 19,840 tons in 1851 to 958 tons in 1870. To balance this, the tonnage to Hull and the coastal trade had dramatically increased from 579 in 1851 to 46,424 in 1870 whilst that to Goole had grown slightly and stood at 24,424 tons in 1870. During this period of its life the Barnsley Canal was in need of costly and constant maintenance due to the silting up of the channel and the large accumulation of weed in some lengths of the cut. The Barugh locks were in a very bad state of repair despite £7,000 being spent on improvements and on 6 August 1861 the scourge of the Barnsley Canal gave notice of its future intentions. On this fateful day the canal bank burst at Royston due to subsidence and deposited a loaded sloop, complete with her crew, in a field some four hundred yards away. During the three weeks it took to reopen the canal over one hundred boats were queueing up to continue their journeys. The sinking of the land as a result of coal extraction from beneath the canal was eventually to lead to its downfall; banks had to be continually strengthened and the channel dredged to overcome the changing contours of the canal bed. In 1866, according to an entry in the Barnsley Canal Minute Book of 4 July, the committee went to inspect the aqueduct and reported considerable damage caused by the sinking of the land. Great caution was required in preventing both the fissures in the rock and the cracks in the arches of the aqueduct becoming larger. However, the Aire & Calder still had faith in the Barnsley when between 1879 and 1881 they lengthened all the locks up to Barugh from the original 66 feet to 84 feet but leaving the width at 15 feet in an attempt to accommodate the newer 79 feet long barges of iron construction that were now taking the place of the wooden-built keels, though some boat builders remained faithful to wood for many years to come.

By 1893 the five locks and the canal above Barugh wharf had been abandoned when maintenance costs far outweighed the tolls received from the scant trade on this section of the canal due to the monopoly of the railway serving the Silkstone coalfield.

The second major breach occurred on 20 November 1911 when the embankment adjacent to the aqueduct failed because of the ever present subsidence and caused the closure of the canal until 10 July 1912. The

Pulley wheels mounted on stone or concrete blocks were used on many of the tighter bends in the Barnsley Canal. Situated near the apex, the horse marine would run the towing rope around the pulley to maintain the correct angle of the rope in relation to the barge. There are very few left now but they can be found.

With the construction of the Wintersett reservoir, in 1854, to supplement water supplies to the canal, a beam engine pump was installed to lift water from the Cold Hiendley reservoir into the new one. Commissioned in 1874, this engine, by Harvey's of Hale, pumped water into a narrow feeder that ran alongside the original reservoir into the canal. This feeder was also used to convey coal and other goods to service the steam plant; due to the restricted width of the feeder a narrow boat was used for this task.

following graphic account appeared in the *Barnsley Chronicle* of Saturday 25 November 1911:

> *A miner named Oscar Cooper, of Harborough Hills, was on the spot when the water began to break through. He was taking a short cut, about 5.30 in the morning, to get to his work at the Barnsley Main Colliery, when he noticed water working itself through the banks. He crept back and warned other colliers who were following. They considered it dangerous to attempt to cross* [the aqueduct] *and Cooper went to call the canal bank man. The water rapidly increased in volume, and at ten minutes to six the men saw the bank collapse. Cooper says, 'There was a rumble like thunder, and then the bank all came down'. A man named Sykes, who lives at the lock house close at hand, says that between five and six he was awakened by a rumbling noise, and went out to see what was the matter. On getting out on the bank he heard a sharp crack. He saw that the bank had given way, but at the time according to his estimate, the breach was not more than five feet wide. The water, however, was making short work of the soft earth; soon the clay puddling in the bed of the canal gave way and before long the gap had extended fifty yards. A long stretch of the canal, estimated at about twelve miles, was draining away through the gap with terrible force. Again, in September 1922, the canal was closed for four months during a severe drought. Despite the trials and tribulations the canal trade held up reasonably well with the total tonnage peaking in 1895/99 at 257,798 and in the four years leading to the outbreak of war had fallen to 192,406 tons. Between the wars traffic steadily declined, mainly due to the collieries along the line being worked out.*

A breach close to the aqueduct on 13 June 1945 caused the flooding of Mottram Wood Colliery and the resultant compensation cost the company £2,375; a sum it could ill-afford. This leak was repaired but by November the general manager was warning of further trouble in the area of the aqueduct where the subsiding ground was forcing the banks to be built higher and higher to maintain a navigable depth of water. Exactly a year later, on 22 November 1946, the canal burst at Littleworth which caused 53 million gallons of water to flood the fields and a nearby housing estate. This time compensation was set at £3,500 and made the Aire & Calder consider the viability of the Barnsley Canal.

In January 1947 a Bill was put before Parliament applying for the nationalisation of the Aire & Calder and this opportunity was taken by the board of directors to recommend the abandonment of the Barnsley waterway. The ministry consented and abandonment was applied for under the Railway & Canal Traffic Act of 1888. The last boat passed through Royston on 7 December 1950 and 10 June 1952 saw the last one to use Heath Lock with the warrant being finally granted in 1953.

The canal quickly deteriorated with the aqueduct being demolished as being 'unsafe' very shortly after closure with the earth's surface compensating for the havoc wreaked far below. The demand for the commodity that had built the Barnsley Canal had finally destroyed it.

The waterway languished in a very sorry state for many years until, in 1984, the Barnsley Canal Group was formed with the intention of highlighting the plight of this piece of our heritage and campaigning for its restoration and return to navigable status, along with the Dearne & Dove Canal.

In Royston the B6428 Midland Road crossed the canal by a very fine lift bridge. It replaced the conventional masonry one in 1934 and was driven by electricity. Control was managed from the cabin mounted on the side and the motors and lift gear located in the very fine and substantial corner towers.

Cliffe Lane Bridge near Cundy Cross is seen in a poor state of repair sometime in the 1960s. At some point cast iron supports have been placed between the abutments to carry the decking after the removal or possibly the collapse of the stonework.

This later picture shows the even greater decline of Cliffe Lane Bridge. Also known as Bayldon Bridge, its demolition is almost complete

The canal bed near Cliffe Lane has fared no better. Nature has very nearly reclaimed the whole width and depth of the channel.

This is the railway viaduct that crossed the Dearne Valley at Hoyle Mill carrying the Barnsley to Cudworth line over the LNER metals on the Stairfoot Curve and the Barnsley Canal. Of tubular steel trestle construction, it survived until the mid-1960s.

A long distance shot taken from the viaduct in February 1954 showing the canal aqueduct crossing the railway and the River Dearne. In the background can be seen the chimneys of Redfearns Glass on the left and the Star Paper Mill to the right. *Norman Marshall.*

The aqueduct adjacent to the junction of the Barnsley Canal and the Dearne & Dove Canal was the finest piece of architecture on the canal. The proprietors were so proud of it that they used it as the company logo on all the stationery and toll tickets. Seen here from the west side, the houses on the horizon are in Monk Bretton.

The aqueduct from the east showing the majestic sweep of the five arches.

On 20 November 1911, the aqueduct suffered a breach on the south abutment that closed the canal for eight months. The junction house can be seen at the back. (See page 18 for a full account).

A further view of the destruction caused by the force of uncontrolled water. It proved a seven day wonder to the local populace that flocked along to see the devastation.

All the water has now gone and an inspection team has got a ladder in place to assess the damage. A policeman keeps a watchful eye on proceedings and a safety fence has been erected. The river took the force of the water and the railway, as can be seen, escaped unscathed.

In the Spring of 1954 the council, in their wisdom, pronounced the aqueduct to be unsafe and commenced to destroy it. The following pictures, taken by Norman Marshall, display the tremendous effort required to demolish the structure. The first photograph shows the drained trough ready for the contractors to begin.

Here an excavator and dump truck are in action. The parapet and trough have gone from the first two arches.

A few days later...

A flag man stands by to warn traffic of impending blasting. The spoil heaps of Barnsley Main Colliery can be seen through the arch.

An empty coal train with the locomotive blowing off steam cautiously approaches the half demolished aqueduct.

Now that the ball and chain can do no further damage, the contractors resort to even tougher methods to dispose of the 'unsafe' structure.

The two men are preparing a blasting charge and the detonator wire can be seen suspended between the remains of the piers. Their efforts have alreay produced a good pile of spoil.

The charge is detonated and a bit more of our heritage disappears.

All the arches are now gone. The scene from the dammed off stop-lock.

This is what now remains of the once proud symbol of the Barnsley Canal.
A wooden walk-way was subsequently laid across the piers which allows
them to play a reduced but still useful role today.

Carrying on along the canal and the junction with its house is located just over the aqueduct. The Dearne & Dove Canal enters from the left.

The junction looking towards the Stop Lock and the Dearne & Dove Canal.

The stop-lock in happier times. The railway can be seen behind the house with a signal box to the left and the viaduct to the right.

Following closure in 1942 of the Dearne & Dove Canal, the stop-lock was de-commissioned to preserve the water in the Barnsley Canal. Here is the stop-lock with stop planks in position and a makeshift sluice suspended on steel girders.

Shortly after the junction, at about 11 miles from the Calder, was
Redfearn's Glass Work's original site. After the closure of the canal the firm
moved to a site between Monk Bretton and Cudworth. This picture shows
the wharf at the Glass Works with several barges either unloading or
awaiting cargoes.

Redfearn's wharf looking
towards Harborough Hill
Road, again busy with barge
traffic.

Here the wharf is viewed from under Harborough Hill Road Bridge.

Following the closure of the canal and Redfearn's move, the wharf rapidly deteriorated. The remains of a sunken barge lies among the reeds. In the distance is Harborough Hill Road Bridge and the covered hoist of Redfearn's former warehouse.

Some time later and the barge has sunk even further. The concrete sleepers are all that remains of the track that carried the wharf cranes.

A view of the backs of houses in Twibell Street also showing the chimney of the Star Paper Works. This scene was photographed from the derelict Redfearn's wharf.

Almost the same view as before but the chimneys have now gone. However, the surrounding warehouses and factories appear to have survived.

Harborough Hills Road Bridge viewed from the west showing Redfearn's two chimneys.

A barge load of very happy people being taken on a trip by water and embarking at Old Mill Lane Bridge: probably employees of the glass works on a day out. The barge is of riveted iron construction that was typical of the early 1900s.

A steel-constructed tanker barge unloads petrol at Twibell Street. On the other bank a clinker-built wooden craft is making use of a dockside crane. Old Mill Bridge is in the background.

The same wharf as the previous picture clearly shows the covered gantry for loading and unloading goods from the warehouse.

This peaceful scene is taken from the towpath beneath Old Mill Bridge. The massive stone copings and setts are clearly illustrated.

Many years later and the canal has now been filled in between Harborough Hill Road and Old Mill Lane which became part of the car park for BLMC agents Appleyards. The wall of the former Redfearn's wharf still retains the original mooring rings. The swinging hoist is still in situ on the corner of the warehouse.

The *Keel Inn*, which was built at the canal side, was a popular watering hole for the barge crews. It is one of two 'Keel Inns' on the Barnsley canals, the other being on the Dearne & Dove at Stairfoot.

Looking westwards from near the *Keel Inn* and two barges, a clinker-built and a steel hulled one, are moored at what seems to be a timber yard. This stretch of towpath was well used judging by the provision of a gas street lamp at the junction of the two paths.

Wildfowl sail serenely by the skeleton of a wooden barge that was abandoned when the canal was closed. These remains were left to decay close to the *Keel Inn*.

The Star Paper Mill wharf, viewed from the west, with Old Mill Lane Bridge in the distance. Redfearn's chimneys can be seen behind to the left.

The Star wharf again, photographed from Old Mill Lane Bridge, with several laden and empty barges waiting at the dock. Many bales of paper are stacked up to the rear of the wharf awaiting shipment.

A similar view to the previous one, probably taken after the closure of the canal, with two derelict barges lying in the shallows. Despite the unkempt state of the wharf, the unloading booms are still in place overhanging the water.

A hand-operated crane on the paper mill wharf. The main haulage rope is missing as is the ballast weight. The chimney behind displays the prominent white star emblem of the Star Paper Mill.

Known as the 'Thirty Two Steps' bridge this footway crossed the canal some thirteen and a half miles from the Calder and a mile from Low Barugh. In this picture it is seen being used for a family portrait and all the subjects appear to be in their Sunday best for the occasion.

Another shot of the footbridge that shows its very solid construction. It was eventually replaced by a lower structure.

At Barugh Mill, adjacent to the top of the flight of five locks the River Dearne was weired and a mill pond formed. This powered a water wheel and also was a supply of water to the canal. In the photograph, taken in 1949, can be seen the remains of the wheel and the sluice paddle gear.

A further picture from 1949 showing the mill pond and the remains of the leat. The two sluices that formerly led to the canal can be clearly seen. In the background can be made out the *Millers Inn* advertising Oakwell Ales.

CHAPTER TWO

The Dearne & Dove Canal

Introduction

The road system in the West Riding of Yorkshire during the late eighteenth century was in a parlous state. The situation rapidly became an embarrassment to the Don Navigation Company after the opening of their waterway to Tinsley, near Sheffield. A trans-shipment depot had been established at Swinton for the transfer of goods to and from the district of Barnsley. They were now in the difficult position of having an efficient and convenient method of taking merchandise up to and away from Swinton and an inefficient and highly inconvenient system of horses and carts on mud tracks for the remaining nine and a half miles.

As early as 1773, the Marquis of Rockingham had tentatively pursued the idea of making the River Dearne navigable towards Barnsley, but nothing came of his deliberations. It was not until 1792 that during a shareholders' meeting of the Don Navigation Company the subject was raised once again. This meeting agreed to a proposal that a cut be made from Tinsley up to Sheffield and also resolved to create a canal to Barnsley. It was now imperative that a sensible means of transport was provided to serve the blossoming coal mining and iron working industries of this area. Time was of the essence to the Don Navigation Company as the Aire & Calder Navigation to the north were already making a survey based on their intention to build a canal from Wakefield to Barnsley and then on to Barugh. Consequently, it was only three weeks later that another shareholders' meeting was convened. There it was agreed that a subsidiary company be formed that would be responsible for a navigable cut 'from the river up to Barnsley', and would be made for about £50,000; Robert Whitworth Snr was asked to do the survey under William Jessop's supervision.

Barnsley was now in the fortunate position of having two proposed canals heading towards the town. Much horse-trading ensued between the two companies with regard to branch lines, tolls and water supplies. When both routes had been settled, the required Acts of Parliament were applied for and both were granted on the same day in June 1793.

The Dearne & Dove Canal was to run for nine miles and five furlongs from Swinton through Wath upon Dearne and Wombwell until finally meeting the Barnsley Canal at Hoyle Mill. Two branches were to be built, one to Elsecar of two miles one and a half furlongs and another to Worsbrough of the same length. There would be nineteen locks on the main line, lifting the canal through 127 feet from the River Don. Six locks were needed on the Elsecar branch to lift it forty-eight feet to the terminus basin. Two reservoirs were

Lock number 1 at Swinton where the Dearne & Dove Canal leaves the Sheffield and South Yorkshire Navigation. Despite having been abandoned for many years, the lock gates and walls have been well maintained. The lower four locks and pounds are now occupied by Waddington's boatyard.

Pictured in 1949, lock 2 is in excellent condition and the pound has a good level of water. Sheffield-size barges can be seen moored at both sides of the pound and also in the entrance to the canal below lock 1. The photograph clearly shows the paddle arrangement used throughout the canal with ground paddles at the head of the lock and gate paddles on the tail. The mixed goods train beyond is on the Rawmarsh line of the old South Yorkshire Railway.

planned, at Elsecar and Worsbrough, and one tunnel of 472 yards near Adwick on Dearne.

By December 1798 the canal was open to Elsecar and carrying started from the colliery at once. This early revenue was very welcome as the company was experiencing a shortage of funds due to increased construction costs and unforseen works. On 12 November 1804 the stop-lock leading to the Barnsley Canal was was flooded and the Dearne & Dove declared open. The waterway could accommodate craft fifty-eight feet long by fourteen feet ten inches wide drawing four feet six inches. These dimensions were somewhat less than the those of boats capable of passing locks of the Don Navigation right up to Sheffield.

By this time the Barnsley Canal had been open for almost three years and had managed to build up a good trade. However, when the Dearne & Dove became operational, nearly half the tonnage shipped from Barnby Basin, which was the terminus of the Barnsley Canal some four and a half miles north-west from Hoyle Mill, was soon travelling down the new canal. After settling down, the two companies worked together in reasonable harmony for several years. Any changes in tolls were agreed between them, and the Barnsley, always suffering from water shortage, was supplied from the Worsbrough reservoir between the months of December 1804 and February 1805 with water that was surplus to the Dearne & Dove's needs. This generous offer was not repeated as the Dearne & Dove was itself stopped for lack of water during the summers of 1805 and 1806. An attempt was made to alleviate the situation in 1826 by increasing the depth of Worsborough reservoir by four feet six inches and the acreage from twenty to forty-two.

In 1810 the first dividend paid to the shareholders was 4.46% and in the same year 2,334 boats used the canal. By 1828 almost 150,000 tons of cargo, mainly coal, had been sent down the Dearne & Dove to the tide-way and, all in all, the canal was proving to be quite prosperous. Then the bane of canals raised its head of steam and rolled along the Dearne valley. The North Midland Railway opened in 1840: so in 1845 the Don Navigation Company, trying to protect its trade, tried to buy both the Barnsley and Dearne & Dove canals. The deal for the Barnsley Canal fell through and eventually it was leased to the Aire & Calder Navigation Company. The Dearne & Dove, however, was taken over by the Don Navigation on 1 January 1846.

For the next forty years the canal continued to serve the coalfields of the Barnsley area with fluctuating fortunes. Various tactics were used to coax traffic away from the Barnsley Canal in order to make the waterway viable in the face of railway competition. During these years the parent company was involved in many attempted take-overs and amalgamations as the railways increased their stranglehold on the region's transport system. In 1889 they were in the ownership of the Manchester, Sheffield & Lincolnshire Railway Company when an Act of Parliament was obtained enabling an operating company to be set up governing all four of South Yorkshire's canals. These were the Sheffield Canal, the Don Navigation, the Stainforth & Keadby and the Dearne & Dove. The company so formed took the now familiar name of the Sheffield & South Yorkshire Navigation Company.

Barges moored between locks two and three at Swinton. *City of Sheffield,*
on the left, is a wooden hulled Sheffield size craft that was capable of
navigating the Dearne & Dove Canal, the Barnsley Canal and the flight of
locks giving access to Sheffield Basin that were built only fifty-seven feet
long.

The first bridge over this waterway carries the A6022 Mexborough to
Swinton road. Also known as Halmshaw Bridge it crosses the canal at the
head of lock 4. Despite the ravages caused by the boatyard, this scene can
still be recognised today.

Five years previously, the industry which had given the Dearne & Dove its prosperity began to exact payment as the first sign of the cause of the canal's demise started to appear. A twenty-five yard section of banking on the Worsbrough Branch collapsed due to subsidence from the colliery workings nearby. It took six months and £19,000 to restore the canal to navigation. This, however, was only the beginning; in 1906 the situation in this part of the coalfield was so bad that the Worsbrough Branch was closed completely because of unsupportable maintenance costs due to land settlement. Following this closure, the company reluctantly agreed to allow the extraction of coal from directly below the canal thus effectively signing its death warrant.

In 1928 the Elsecar Branch was also closed due to subsidence and the high costs involved in protecting the navigation. It became increasingly difficult to maintain a navigable depth of water in the main line and in 1934 the last boat made the passage to Barnsley. The Dearne & Dove Canal was now closed except for a short length at either end. By 1942 the same malady had closed the Barnsley Canal as well and in a further ten years the remaining traffic on the Dearne & Dove, from Manvers Main Colliery at Wath to the Don ceased. Final abandonment came in 1961 apart from the first four locks which were kept open by back pumping to serve Waddington's boat yard and a local glass works. The Barnsley Canal had received its abandonment warrant some years previously, in 1953.

After closure the infrastructure of the canal continued to be affected by the land settlement and many bridges were lowered when they became unsafe. The main industries of this region, coal and glass, were still in a state of development and land was needed for expansion and development. The canal which ran close by was a ready source of such land which was greedily swallowed up.

Fortunately, a photographic record was made of the Dearne & Dove before almost 70 per cent of the main line disappeared totally. Many of the pictures that follow depict the canal during this twilight period with most of the features still intact but sadly neglected.

In 1984 the newly formed Barnsley Canal Group started to campaign for the restoration of both the Barnsley Canal and the Dearne & Dove Canal. With the help of various grants and hard working volunteers, they managed to bring the terminus basin and top pound of the Elsecar branch back into a navigable state. This canal society, re-named the Barnsley and Dearne & Dove Canals Trust is still carrying on the work today.

Immediately prior to lock 5 the the former North Midland Railway metals cross the canal before heading off into Swinton station. The signal box, named Swinton Junction, controlled the junction of the branch to the South Yorkshire Railway main line.

This picture of locks 5 and 6 clearly shows the 'over-spill' method of water control used on this canal. Instead of going to the expense of by-washes, the Don Navigation Company opted for the cheaper way of letting excess water gravitate down the waterway. To have this amount of excess water on the Dearne & Dove would have been very welcome during its operating days. Nothing now remains of the locks or canal in this vicinity.

Lock 6 is displaying an artificially maintained low water level in the chamber due to the top boards on the gates having been removed. This does, however, show the construction methods of the lock chamber with brickwork sides being capped with stone copings. Also clearly shown is the mechanism used to raise the gate paddle when filling the lock.

Here, only a furlong north of lock 6, the canal runs in company with the South Yorkshire Railway and both are crossed by the quite imposing four-arch North Midland Railway viaduct. The rather motley collection of coal wagons are heading for Barnsley. Until 1840 this cutting was the site of the 472 yard long Adwick Tunnel which was opened out and the canal re-aligned to accommodate the rails of the new railway.

Just a few yards further on from the previous picture and we are still in the cutting. Recent repair work has taken place to preserve the canal bank and possibly to protect the railway embankment from slippage. This work would have been made necessary by subsidence.

The canal is here shown in 1954 still in water but very much reduced in depth and width. Adwick Road bridge can be seen in the distance and Manvers Main Colliery is on the right. The railway wagons are on part of the very extensive colliery sidings.

Taken only five years earlier, this picture shows
Adwick Road bridge in greater detail. A dumb
work boat is moored on the far side of the
channel which shows that maintenance work
was still being carried out at this time. This
bridge has since been destroyed and the canal
line has disappeared under warehousing.

This canalside warehouse to
the south of Wath is seen in
1954 overlooking a very reedy
canal

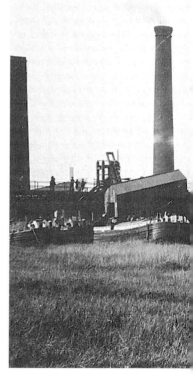

Here we see *Alice*, an iron-hulled barge, being loaded with tar from Manvers Main at Wath in 1950. Whilst loading is taking place the skipper, Jim Rawnsley, and his mate retire to the pit canteen.

This undated print, taken from a postcard, shows the canal very busy with no less than four barges attending Manvers Main Colliery. The craft on the right is clearly a wooden-built barge that has all its curved hatch covers in place.

Doncaster Road, Wath, in the early part of the twentieth century and repair work is taking place on a drainage system along the towpath of the canal. Manvers Main can be seen on the right. A new Doncaster Road was eventually built on the filled - in line of the canal but the original still exists as a service road. Hatfield's clothing shop is next door to a fish and chip shop, while on the next corner is a general store advertising Cadbury's Chocolate, Hudson's Soap, Colman's Starch and Colman's Mustard.

The same location as the previous picture but taken from the other direction in 1949. Again, repair work is taking place but this time on the opposite bank. The derelict state of the channel is well illustrated. Common Bridge can be seen at the end of the visible channel.

Common Bridge in 1948 where Doncaster Road, the former A6023 Mexborough to Wath road, crossed the canal.

Shortly after Common Bridge the oil works of Chas Stanley was located. Seen here in the late nineteenth century a visiting sloop is loading barrels of oil. The mast is probably stepped in order to check the rigging as a craft could only be bow-hauled to this stretch of canal with its many low bridges.

The canal channel to the north of Common Bridge looking south. Manvers Main is seen in the distance.

Looking north to Station Road bridge in Wath. The utility crossing the bridge is possibly water using a very complex riveted box section pipe over the canal. The beautifully shaped arch stones can be clearly seen in this picture.

Taken from Station Road bridge and looking east, this photograph from 1951 shows the sweep of the canal as it leaves Common Bridge some two miles from Swinton. A contractor's van and workmen are at work on the towpath.

The next feature of the canal is Outlane Swing Bridge which is here seen in the distance. There would appear to have been some quite drastic pruning done to the trees and bushes on the far side of the channel.

Outlane Swing Bridge pictured from the easten side in 1954. The channel here is very choked with reeds and the water level is low.

A closer view of Outlane Bridge which shows the central pivot point quite clearly.The traffic barriers at either end can also be seen still in situ, though many years have passed since they held up any impatient travellers while a barge navigated this length of waterway.

This rare picture, taken in 1949, shows a fine footbridge that was erected to allow the workers convenient access to Wath Brewery. The angled abutments display the consideration given by the canal builders to the clearest passage along the towpath for the barge horses.

At this point the canal swung sharply northwards on an embankment in order to cross a valley and avoid the main village of Wath which, even in the late 1700s, was quite populous. This feature became known as 'The Bay of Biscay' due to the breadth of the canal at this point. The name is still to be found where part of the B6097 in Wath is called 'Biscay Way'. Brook Dike, a stream which ran through the village was divereted under the embankment by a feature known as the 'Double Culverts'. This photograph shows the stream exiting the culverts on the south side of the embankment.

Here the north entrance to the 'Double Culverts' is pictured in 1952. The tunnel on the left would apear to have been converted into a footpath with the dike relegated to the other.

Having returned to a more westerly direction the canal now passes under Wet Moor Bridge just three miles from Swinton. This picture again demonstrates the well designed purpose-built bridges on this canal.

Shortly after Wet Moor Bridge, the canal runs close to Wath marshalling yard. When the Dearne & Dove was opened in 1804 the railway was nowhere to be seen and the canal prospered. Then, in 1849, the North Midland Railway arrived and very soon the canal profits dwindled. This photograph from 1949 illustrates the derelict canal and the ever bustling railway sitting side by side.

Factory Bridge shows the builder's design for an accommodation bridge on this canal. The abutments still display the double stringer courses so effectively used in the arched bridges but the decking is totally utilitarian.

Pictured here in 1948 is Old Moor Bridge which carries the B6273, Brampton to Darfield road, over the canal. The concrete reinforcement to the towpath bank of the canal can be clearly seen. Also still in situ is the balk of timber on the corner of the abutment that prevented the ropes from horse drawn barges cutting grooves into the stonework. In this photograph the towpath is passable and the brige decking has a tired and care-worn appearance.

This shows Old Moor Bridge one year later in 1949 from the other side and it is now sporting a new decking. To give additional strength to the deck supports have been taken from the concrete edgings and the towpath rendered unusable. Hence the very elaborate construction on the right designed to carry the right of way up to road level and, presumably, a similar stairway is provided at the other side.

Well Spring lock, number 7, is pictured with Wombwell in the background. Once again, the top boards have been removed from the head gates to lower the water level. This is the lowest lock of the Brampton four and empties into a three and a quarter mile long pound stretching to lock 6 at Swinton. This length of water necessitated an overflow which was provied just before Old Moor Bridge and flowed into Knoll Beck that ran very close by at this point.

The A633 Barnsley to Rotherham road crosses the canal over Knoll Beck Bridge which, like all traces of the canal hereabouts, have disappeared completely. This photograph shows what seems to be an obstruction built across the towpath beneath the bridge.

Quarry Lock, number 8, seen here in 1948 with a vey low water level being maintained. The wing wall on the left is showing signs of imminent collapse.

This railway lift bridge, located between locks 8 and 9 at Brampton, carried the single line South Yorkshire Railway extension to Elsecar New Colliery. Pictured in 1948, the structure appears intact and has a full compliment of balancing and lifting chains. The abuments to the right are for the aqueuct that took the canal over Knoll Beck at this point.

Viewed from the other side, this scene shows the Lift Bridge with a loaded coal train crossing the canal. A gate seems to have been constructed across the towpath to perhaps deter people from crossing the line.

Taken in 1954, this picture shows the speed at which the canal channel has deteriorated. It also shows in greater clarity the 'South Yorkshire' motif cast into the iron headworks of the bridge.

The tail of lock 9 at Brampton is pictured in 1949. The force with which the water is leaking through the gate signifies a good head of water being held in the chamber. The discharge from a pipe in the left-hand wing wall will be from a land drain or spring that was culverted.

Lock 10 and the Wombwell Junction of the main line and the Elsecar branch in 1948. The main line carries on to the right passing through Junction Bridge. A wooden mooring post has survived as well as a stable block on the right.

Junction Bridge carrying the A633 over the canal at Brampton. The ramp at the right-hand side gives access to the road above.

Everill Gate Lane crossed the canal by means of Everill Gate Bridge seen here in 1948. The gas lamp stanard can be clearly seen on the road.

The very grandly named Double Bridges was in fact an access bridge that also carried a pipe over the canal. The gasometer that supplied Wombwell can be seen on the extreme right of the picture.

Reproduced from an old postcard, this scene shows Station Road Bridge in Wombwell carrying the B6096 Darfield to Wombwell road.

A closer view of Station Road Bridge showing the ornate balustrading, with ornamental embelishments in the middle, mounted on newer abutments that were provided when the bridge was widened.

Littlefield Lane crossed the canal by means of this access bridge.

The first railway bridge at Aldham carried the Barnsley and Sheffield Branch of the South Yorkshire Railway over the canal. Seen here photographed from the south, with Aldham Bridge in the background, the typical Dearne & Dove stonework is well illustrated.

Bradbury Balk Lane, connecting Wombwell to Low Valley, was carried over the canal by this beautifully built bridge, sadly demolished in 1985. The chimney showing over the right hand side parapet belongs to Mitchell Main Colliery. The pipe crossing the bridge is carrying coal gas that was produced in the coke ovens at Mitchell Main.

Looking south from the rail bridge gives an excellent view of the Mitchell Main Colliery in 1948.

The second brige at this complicated junction of canal, road, rail and river, is Aldham Bridge that carries the A633 over the canal once again. The effects of subsidence can be seen here, with the towpath almost under water and the shoring props on the abutment walls. Lock 11 is just beyond the bridge.

Lock 11, the first of the Stairfoot flight, is viewed from under Aldham Bridge. Dereliction and subsidence are rife in this picture, with the broken balance beams and gates. As well as the towpath being submerged the wing walls are rapidly disappearing. The ruins behind the lock are what was left of the Aldham Corn Mill.

Shortly after lock 11 the canal crossed the River Dearne by this three-arched aqueuct.

This rail bridge carried a branch of the South Yorkshire Railway over the canal shortly before lock 12. Taken in 1949, the picture shows that the canal bed is all but silted up and infested with reeds. This point is seven miles from Swinton.

Lock 12 on the Stairfoot flight, pictured in 1948, has fared better than the previous one and the gates are in good condition with paddle gear and hand rails still in place.

Taken in 1949, this photograph shows lock 13 with the wing walls in a decrepit condition. The gates are ajar displaying the very low water level in the chamber and the pound. However, the channel here is still quite clear and well defined

The right hand bottom gate of lock 14 has lost its balance beam and the wing walls have started to fall away. The width of the canal between these two locks, which are only a few yards apart, served both as a passing place for keels and as a reservoir for the volume of water each barge brought down with it before filling the next lock down.

Locks 15 and 16 show the closeness of the locks on the Stairfoot flight. Although the gates are in a bad state, the lock chamber walls and the cill are very well preserved.

This picture of locks 16 and 17 shows that these head gates are holding back quite a head of water and, judging by the overspill, a fair amount is flowing down the canal. The group of children are enjoying using the derelict canal as a playground.

Top lock of the Stairfoot flight, number 18, and the ruined mill that stood on the junction with the Worsbrough branch. This branch left the main line to the left of the picture behind the mill buildings and the toll-booth.

Looking back down the Stairfoot flight from the top lock. Mitchell's Main can be seen in the distance as well as the previous rail bridge. The young lady is resting on the balance beam of the tail gate of top lock.

Caulk Lane crossed the canal by means of this nicely proportioned but rather high bridge. The towpath beneath the bridge appears to have been built up for some reason, giving a discrepancy in heights with the wing wall on the opposite bank.

This railway bridge crossed the canal just south of Stairfoot at a point just eight miles from Swinton. The LMS locomotive and brake van are seen in 1949. Close by, *The Keel* public house was canalside; it is now the only reminder that a canal once played its part in this community.

Two views of Doncaster Road Bridge carrying the A635 over the canal. Taken five years apart, the stop-planks are still in place holding back quite a head of water.

Only a few yards after the Doncaster Road Bridge is found the first rail bridge north of Stairfoot. Viewed in 1949, the towpath wall looks to be in perfect condition. The gentleman on the right appears to be sporting a pair of plus-four trousers.

Thomlinson's Glassworks, Stairfoot, as it looked in 1954 with two working kilns. The channel here is virtually choked with reeds and weed.

The next rail bridge to cross the canal was situated just before the Beatson & Clark glassworks. Shown here in 1949, the works can be seen through the bridge.

A longer view taken in 1954 of Beatson & Clark's glassworks. During the intervening years the reed infestation would appear to have subsided to some degree. A fence would seem to have been erected across the canal and towpath, though it does not appear to have been much of a problem to the small boy and his companion!

This carefully posed photograph of Ryland's Glass & Engineering Works, now Beatson & Clark, shows a scene of great activity with nothing happening. The men unloading the coal barge have a fully laden kibble ready whilst the crane driver leans on his cab door and surveys the world. The other workers appear frozen and all are looking directly at the camera. Barnsley Main Colliery can be seen beyond the gantry.

Taken in 1949, this view shows Barnsley Main Colliery with the canal running past and its channel completely reed bound. The Barnsley to Cudworth railway crosses the canal and passes by the colliery between the head gear and the associated coking plant. To the right can be seen the LNER rails crossing the A628 Pontefract Road. In the background are the five arches of the Barnsley Canal aqueduct over the railway and the River Dearne.

Oaks Lane Bridge carries the road of that name over the canal. Again, pictured in 1949, the low water level and high amount of debris can be seen. Through the arch is the terrace of Ash Row whilst beyond can be seen Oakwell Brewery and the bobbin makers Beevor Works.

Taken from the other side of Oaks Lane Bridge, the railway viaduct at Barnsley Main is quite visible.

The A 628 crosses the canal for the last time by Beevor Bridge. The chimney of the works can be seen behind the parapet.

At almost ten miles from Swinton, the last engineering feature of the Dearne & Dove Canal is the Junction Lock. This 'lock' was built with cills facing both ways to enable gates to be fitted that prevented any flow of water in either direction. Theoretically the water levels in this and the Barnsley Canal were the same; but each jealously guarded its own water. The lengthesman's house is situated on the junction of the two canals with the Dearne & Dove behind it.

Junction Lock seen in around 1953 in a state of complete ruin. At sometime a sluice has been installed across the head but any need of such a device has long since disappeared along with the water.

CHAPTER THREE

Elsecar Branch

The following photographs of the Elsecar Branch, taken in the 1950s, show a dramatic decline in the condition of the canal. The forlorn subject of the pictures, taken by an unknown photographer, depict a small part of a once mighty network of canals that carried the raw materials that allowed the Industrial Revolution to flourish.

Taken from the junction with the main line, here is seen Brampton Road Bridge that carries the B6089 Wombwell to Rotherham road over the canal.

Shown from the upstream side, Brampton Road Bridge has now got a dam across the channel. A Yorkshire Traction bus crosses over the frozen waters of the canal, travelling towards Rotherham.

Caught in the same cold spell, this desolate length of canal was photographed between Smithy Bridge Lock and Lundhill Bridge.

Warmer weather and the remains of Smithy Bridge Lock looks very
tranquil. Part of the head-gates and a mooring stud have just survived.

Just over one mile from the junction and Storey Lock is in desperate straits. In the distance can be seen Tingle Bridge.

The head-gates of Storey Lock looking downstream. The chamber wall is still in very good condition despite the ravages of nature.

The view downstream from Tingle Bridge looking towards Storey Lock. The channel has all but disappeared and only a trickle of water marks the route of the canal.

Tingle Bridge Lock seen from Tingle Bridge. To the right of this picture is
the *Elephant & Castle* public house. This small section of the canal was
restored in 1986, when the channel was dredged and the lock walls
repaired.

Hemingfield Basin is located about 200 yards upstream of Tingle Bridge
and was built to serve the nearby colliery. This photograph shows the
bridge over the entrance cut leading into the wharves.

Here can be seen the entrance to the basin and the layout of the wharves edged by the railings. At the rear of the basin was an overspill into Knoll Beck which was culverted through the area.

A wider view showing the extent of Hemingfield Basin and the single-track railway that served Lord Fitzwilliam's workshops and private station.

Elsecar Low Lock was the fourth lock on the branch. This view is taken looking down stream and very little appears to be left of the tail gates though the masonry seems to be intact at least on the towpath side.

Low Lock looking upstream with Cortonwood Colliery in the background.

Cobcar Bridge and lock viewed from a tided up length of canal. The bridge was later lowered and the canal culverted. Elsecar parish church spire is seen behind.

The remains of Cobcar Lock from the upstream side of the bridge.

The head gates of Cobcar Lock are still recognisable at this time and the chamber walls are in reasonable condition. The pipe is a gas main.

Elsecar Top Lock with all four gates in place and the lock walls undamaged. This was soon to change when the locks were cascaded and the walls demolished. A concrete dam was built across the head of Top Lock to maintain a water level in the pound and basin above.

Fifty yards up stream from Top Lock was the overflow sluice for the top
pound of the branch. It discharged into a culvert and re-appeared some one
hundred yards away as Knoll Beck. The sluice chamber is located in front of
the railings in this postcard from the early part of the century which shows
Elsecar Main Colliery with its extensive railway sidings and sign-written
coal wagons. This was a popular place to cool off during hot weather!

Following the closure of the canal in 1928, probably for safety reasons, the
sluice chamber was greatly reduced. The large diameter cement pipes
were installed and the rear of the chamber back-filled. The culvert beyond
this point is a fully stone-lined tunnel.

The top pound has here been photographed from the head gate of Top Lock. The spire of Elsecar church can be seen above the building on the right. Despite the reed growth, there is still a good level of water at this point.

The Elsecar Branch terminus basin looking down stream. The silt and reeds have taken over completely and only a trickle of water now feeds the top pound. Elsecar Main can be seen along with the massive spoil heap behind. This basin was fully dredged and restored in the 1990s by the Barnsley Canal Group.

The Dearne & Dove canal was supplied with water from two reservoirs; one at Worsbrough and the second at Elsecar. Situated alongside Water Lane, the reservoir had been formed by damming Knoll Beck. From here the water was fed by a culvert running under the Fitzwilliam workshops and discharging into the basin. Seen here in 1948, the water level is very low and the rowing boat is 'high and dry'.

The same year and a totally different aspect! A gala atmosphere prevails and *Girl Pat* is busy giving rides to children from a well constructed landing stage. The notice to the right reads: 'Bathing or swimming from this boat or landing stage is strictly prohibited'. The boat would seem to be powered by a quite powerful motor.

CHAPTER FOUR

Worsbrough Branch

The junction of the Worsbrough Branch and the Dearne & Dove. Lock number 18 can be seen behind the pump house. In the distance to the left is Caulk Bridge on the main line. The branch leaves the Dearne & Dove at the rear of the pipe crossing the canal, it then turns sharp left under the footbrige. Here, in 1948, a dam has been constructed across the head to retain water in the main line.

Swaithe Bridge has long since disappeared and the canal is now part of an extensive rubbish tip.

Beyond Swaithe, the Sheffield to Barnsley railway line crosses the canal by means of this high-level viaduct. The channel, seen here in the earlier part of the century, is quite clear and navigable.

The contrast here in 1948 is enormous; the channel is totally dry and only a fraction of its original width. The second deck of the viaduct to the right carries the railway over the River Dearne.

A few hundred yards to the west of the viaduct and the canal is still in very good condition. This picture was taken on the same day as the previous one, in 1948.

Officials from the Sheffield & South Yorkshire and the Aire & Calder Navigations are seen here inspecting Lewden Bridge in April 1948. This bridge carried Station Road over the canal. It is now demolished and lowered.

Pictured here is Goose Hulls Bridge which carries Edmunds Road over the canal at Worsbrough. The *Edmunds Arms* public house is just the other side of the bridge. To the top left of the picture can be seen the upper level of a gasometer.

This ramshackle scene is of Longley's works in Worsbrough who had their own pedestrian bridge across the canal. The sheer-legs appears to be supporting the pipe that is dipping into the water. Though for what purpose?

This view of Worsbrough basin is taken from the footbridge in the previous picture. The chimney in the centre rear belongs to the Worsbrough Mill.

This footbridge, built after the closure of the canal, is situated to the east of Worsbrough basin.

The basin at the head of the branch canal was a popular fishing ground. In this picture, taken in July 1948, it appears that a fishing competition is in progress. The Worsbrough reservoir, located across the A61 road to the left of the photograph, was the main source of water for the canal.

This view of the basin shows the overflow which ran off into the River Dove close by. The weir level at this point had to be raised due to subsidence from the Low Fenton seam of Barrow Colliery.

CHAPTER FIVE

Where Now?

The two waterways rapidly fell into disrepair and final abandonment was granted for the Dearne & Dove Canal in 1961. That for the Barnsley Canal had been obtained some years earlier in 1953.

Following closure, the infrastructure of the canals continued to be affected by land settlement and subsidence which caused many bridges to be lowered as they became unsafe. The main industries in the area, coal and glass, were still developing and land was desperately needed for expansion. The route of both canals had provided a corridor for the growth of the industries and along which the product of these concerns was transported. With the demise of the waterways, the now available land was greedily swallowed up with much of the channel being filled in and used for car parks or the erection of buildings. Along other stretches the canal was used as a convenient rubbish tip for all and sundry to dispose of any unwanted material.

Thus the Dearne & Dove and Barnsley canals languished in abject misery, their once ingeniously engineered channels suffering the indignity of official vandalism. This sorry state of affairs lasted until 1 April 1984 when, following a number of letters in the local press decrying the lack of interest in the waterways, an open meeting was held in the *Royal Hotel* in Barnsley. Formerly known as the *White Bear Hotel*, this was where the inaugural meeting of the shareholders of the Barnsley Canal Company was convened on 15 October 1792. From the 1984 meeting emerged the Barnsley Canal Group with Alan Hall as its chairman; a role he administered with consummate efficiency for over fifteen years.

Once established, the group campaigned tirelessly for the protection of the remaining lengths of the two canals. Gradually a cordial relationship was built up between the group and Barnsley Metropolitan Council who are responsible for much of the canal corridor. During 1989 a partnership was developed between the canal group and the Cortonwood & Elsecar Project. This group was formed with the intention of preserving the former Earl Fitzwilliam's workshops and converting them to a heritage centre. Located at the head of the Elsecar Branch of the Dearne & Dove Canal these buildings, along with a Newcomen beam engine, reverted from National Coal Board ownership to the Council upon the closure of the Cortonwood Colliery.

The canal group was anxious to find a length of waterway that could be physically restored to demonstrate the viability of complete restoration of both canals. The terminus basin at Elsecar was identified as an ideal starting point and, following necessary negotiations, the first working party was held on 4 Februrary 1990.

Unstinting support in the form of man-power and plant was gratefully accepted from the Waterway Recovery Group, the restoration arm of the Inland Waterways Association. Their enthusiasm, experience and resources were invaluable to the canal group at this time and full use of these attributes was made.

The following pictorial account covers the period from the start of restoration to when Elsecar basin had been restored to navigation and other features had been excavated.

Taken in January 1990, this picture shows the overgrown loading wharf and the silted up state of the basin. A large willow tree has managed to establish itself in the centre of the channel.

The first working party cleared three trees, and their stumps, from the edge of the wharf. The damage to the stonework was, fortunately, minimal. Once the vegetation had been removed the stonework was found to be in remarkably good condition.

A great diversity of rubbish was to be found in the abandoned canal. Here the first of several water-logged cable reels is dragged out onto the bank adjacent to Top Lock.

When the basin was first drained down it became obvious that an enormous task lay ahead. Many hundreds of tons of silt would have to be removed in order to attain the depth of water necessary for navigation. The arch that can be seen at the head of the basin is where Knoll Brook enters the canal from the reservoir sited at the far side of the village.

Elsecar Top Lock in 1990. The lock gates had been replaced by a concrete dam to preserve a level of water in the basin and top pound. A sluice and weir, located at the head of the lock, took the surplus water from the basin into a channel that once again became Knoll Beck. After heavy rainfall, however, a considerable amount of water would flow over the dam into what remained of the lock chamber.

Looking downstream from Top Lock towards Cobcar Bridge Lock with the large drainage pipe in view. Beyond this can be seen the gas main that will also have to be diverted to allow headroom for eventual navigation. The amount of debris, vegetation and silt in view makes the work involved in restoration seem very daunting.

The sluice and chamber at Top lock. This is the only way that the basin can be drained whilst work is carried out. The existing wooden gate was very soon replaced by a steel one that was much easier to operate.

In March 1990 a boat was launched on the Dearne & Dove Canal for the first time in decades. The group's work boat was used to assist in attaching a grappling hook onto large pieces of rubbish on the canal bed to enable them to be dragged out.

After launching, the boat proceeds in the direction of Top Lock. Shovels can make excellent paddles when necessary.

Another of the ubiquitous cable reels hooked up prior to being removed from the water. In the foreground a lorry tyre awaits its turn.

A JCB digger is being used to clear out the silt and rubble from the head of Top Lock. The gate reveals and paddle gear grooves can be seen in the wing wall.

In order to facilitate the launching of boats onto the canal, it was decided to build a slipway at the end of the wharf on the basin. Here a JCB makes the initial cut into the canal bank. Elsecar parish church can be seen in the background.

Members of the canal group laying hard-core in readiness for the concrete that will form the base of the slipway.

This picture shows the partially stone-paved section of the slipway that is above the water level.

Prior to the retaining walls being built, the coping stones on the basin edge adjacent to the slipway had to be re-aligned. This was no mean task as the larger stones weighed up to half a ton each.

The finished article with the stone-built abutment walls and heavyweight cast railings. The slipway was a very much appreciated addition to the canal as it allowed many different types of craft to be launched. This became most apparent when the Barnsley Canal Group held their annual 'Trail Boat Rally' on the basin.

September 1991 saw the first Trail Boat Rally to be held at Elsecar. Nine craft, including a Caraboat, were launched, down the as yet unfinished slipway, along with *Elsa*, a trip boat owned by the Cortonwood & Elsecar Project. She was kept busy all weekend carrying passengers down to Top Lock and back.

Elsa prepares to take another load of people along the canal.

Elsa returns from Top lock with another full complement of passengers.

Meanwhile work was continuing on the clearance of Top Lock. In this picture the water is being pumped out before work can commence.

Here, the sheer magnitude of the task is quite apparent. The infill consists of the upper layers of stone blocks from the chamber walls along with glutinous black mud. The 'Elsecar Mud', formed through many years worth of coal falling into the canal, became well known in the waterway restoration world for its clothes staining properties and smell. It was also sold in 1lb jars to raise funds for restoration!

A busy site with work being carried out in the Top Lock and scrub clearance in the next pound. In the foreground a barrow hoist is used to lift loaded barrows out of the chamber.

The crane, a Jones KL15 belonging to the Waterway Recovery Group, is hoisting a kibble that holds around a quarter of a ton which will be emptied into a dumper and taken to the spoil site. In this picture, taken in March 1992, the Mayor of Barnsley, Cllr. Trevor Naylor, is operating the crane on one of his visits to the site when he expressed his support for the restoration scheme.

This picture, taken a week or two later, shows that considerable progress has been made with the lock invert having been cleared for most of the chamber.

Here a volunteer empties a barrow load of silt from the lock chamber. At the end of the day's work, the JCB would disperse and level out the silt in a designated area.

Work was also carried out on the top pound of the canal. Here volunteers are clearing pieces of rubbish from the channel at the head of Top Lock. To the left is the draining sluice.

Channel clearance taking place at the old flour mill wharf halfway along the pound. The kibble is loaded and then ferried across the canal to a dumper on the other bank.

The full kibble arrives to be lifted out of the boat and emptied into a dumper for disposal.

In order to dredge the basin, a machine with a very long reach was needed. To this end a Priestman excavator with a sixty foot reach was hired. Here the large piece of plant arrives in Dawson's yard on its low loader.

The Priestman takes its first bite of the silt in the basin.

A pair of two-ton dumper trucks were kept busy disposing of the silt that was dredged out of the basin.

Clearing the channel at the head of the basin. Shortly after this time, apart from a small island that even this machine could not reach, it was deemed that there was sufficient depth along this stretch of the canal for reasonable navigation.

The remaining island that was removed by hand some weeks later giving the first fully navigable stretch of the Dearne & Dove Canal since closure.

With the help of the same grant, a two-ton Liner dumper was purchased. This replaced the ancient and failing half ton Benford dumper that was on loan from the Waterway Recovery group. It was never to be seen this clean again!

In December 1992 the Group obtained, courtesy of a grant, a Kubota KH31 360° excavator. This versatile machine was found to be much better suited to working in the wet and muddy conditions than the JCB.

The next project was to excavate the pound between Top Lock and Cobcar Bridge Lock. To achieve this, the silt and debris had to be drained and a channel cut to allow any flood water to run away without wetting the whole area. Cobcar Bridge Lock had been cascaded with concrete and the first job was to cut this out to allow drainage.

This picture shows the cascade, the high pressure gas pipe, the drainage pipe and Top Lock in the distance.

A pneumatic drill was used to break out the concrete structure. The infill beneath contained many of the coping stones from the lock chamber walls.

Having broken up the cascade, it then had to be removed from the remains of the lock chamber with crane and dumper assisted by a lot of man (and woman) power.

The first consideration was an access for plant into the pound without interrupting the drainage channel. This was achieved using railway sleepers and concrete drainage pipes.

Construction of the access ramp. Not a total success as the sleepers became very slippery as the mud got on to them.

A layer of pit belting vastly improved the situation and, at last, work could start on the silt removal.

A combination of dumper and crane is being used to clear silt and debris from the tail of Top Lock. It can be seen in the centre foreground that the wing wall of the lock is being exposed.

The drainage channel needed constant deepening to enable the silt to dry out as far down as possible.

Inroads are being made into the silt beds. Here the excavations have reached the large drainage pipe.

130

After many months of hard work the pound is finally cleared. Here a dam is being built in the head of Cobcar Bridge Lock to enable the pound to be flooded for the first time.

Water is being slowly let into the pound from the sluice in Top Lock. The lock cill can be clearly seen in this picture.

More stop planks have been added and the depth is now about three feet. On-going maintenance is required to block up leaks in the dam.

The pound is flooded to the top of the stop planks. The leakage is minimal and the level can easily be maintained from Top Lock.

The first boats on the Cobcar Bridge pound for several decades. The Floating Wardrobe, a canoe and an Amphicat. This scene was part of the 1994 Trail Boat Rally.

Many different craft took part in this very successful event. Here Elsa is busy carrying visitors along the canal amidst a scene of great activity.

A lovely original skiff was launched and provided a touch of bygone charm to the attractions.

The Bell Boats also attended and very soon were giving valuable lessons in team work and water safety to the dozens of visitors that took advantage of the offer to take part.

A traditional jazz band also contributed to a great atmosphere on this extremely enjoyable weekend.

Shortly after the Rally, Barnsley Metropolitan Council landscaped the side of the basin and provided seating in a very attractive seeded area.

In June 1993 the Barnsley Canal Group bought a work boat. This was British Waterways 80285 *Dolphin* which, at fifty feet long and eleven foot six inches wide had been built to work on the keel-sized Barnsley and Dearne & Dove canals. Fitted with a three cylinder Lister diesel engine, she is seen here moored at Elsecar.

Funding was also being sought to install top gates on Top Lock. To allow this to happen one wing wall had to be rebuilt. Many of the original stones had disappeared and new ones had to be cast in concrete that had been coloured to a suitable shade. Here the stonework is being prepared for the reconstruction.

Scaffolding has been erected and the wall is almost complete. The original capping stones have been replaced. Some of these were rescued from the chamber where they had been dumped.

The next area to be considered for restoration was the pound between Cobcar Bridge Lock and Elsecar Low Lock. To obtain access for the necessary plant, a barrier had to be removed, with the blessing of the council, and a ramp built.

The overgrown bushes along the towpath had to be cut back to allow work to proceed. Some years ago the area immediately below Cobcar Bridge had been cleaned up and a dam inserted across the channel holding some twelve inches of water.

Due to the proposed work on this stretch of water, the National Rivers Authority came to the site and cleared the area of its fish population. These were transferred a couple of miles along the canal to Brampton.

At this point the canal channel is very close to Knoll Beck which runs alongside. The tow path was so narrow that remedial work had to be carried out to allow plant in. On the beck side, stone-filled gabions were used to shore up the bank.

On the canal side, piling was employed to create a water-tight seal along the weak spot. A pneumatic pile-driver is driving the piles home. To the right can be seen the dammed off part of the channel and the new access road.

The next lock down, Elsecar Low Lock, had to be tackled in a different way. Scaffolding was erected across the tail of the lock and two barrow hoists were used to feed two dumpers. Here the scaffolding bridge is being put in place.

Elsecar Low Lock before excavation. This picture demonstrates the scale of the deterioration that has taken place along the canal. However, under all the vegetation and silt a lock chamber is still in existence!

The semi-excavated chamber is surveyed by a Waterway Recovery Group volunteer who was leading a week-long restoration camp in Elsecar.

Following on from the clearing out of Low Lock, contractors were brought in and the channel between the two locks was dug out and profiled. This picture shows the canal in water from the lock wing wall to the dam below Cobcar Bridge.

Eventually the head gates were fitted to Top Lock. Made at Callis Mill, near Hebden Bridge, they were measured and installed professionally.

Contemporary paddle gear has also been fitted to the lock; though minus the winding mechanism to deter vandalism.

A planning triumph for the canal group. As a result of negotiations with the planners, this bridge under the Dearne Valley Link Road at Gypsy Marsh is to accommodate the Dearne & Dove Canal channel when restoration arrives here.

This view of the basin should be compared with the picture on page 108. It is an example of what can be achieved with a lot of enthusiasm and volunteer labour. With the support of the local councils responsible for the line of the Barnsley and Dearne & Dove Canals this metamorphosis could be apparent for the whole of the Forgotten Waterways of Yorkshire.

The Barnsley Canal Group has been transformed into the Barnsley and Dearne & Dove Canals Trust and still actively campaigns for the full restoration of the two waterways.

CHAPTER SIX

Personalities

From the first steps of the fledgling work parties to the achievement of some minor, or major, goal that helped the Barnsley Canal Group along the road towards full restoration of the two canals, several 'characters' from the membership were in the thick of it from the beginning. Turning up on Sunday mornings come rain or shine to put in a hard day's work under, usually, very wet, muddy and cold conditions.

The following picture gallery portrays a few of the many people who helped in so many ways to set the ball rolling to rescue the Dearne & Dove and the Barnsley Canal from terminal obscurity. Unfortunately, some of the hardworking members were very good at dodging the camera and their valuable input was not recorded.

(L to R) John Parry, Treasurer; Alan Hall, Chiarman; David Bullock, Secretary.

Alan Hall and Tony Roe collecting weed from the basin.

Richard Knowles, Plant Officer.

On the left, Roger Glister, Publicity Officer and Tim Wade, Editor, *The Keel* magazine.

Allan Horne descends into the lock.

(L to R) Geof Coates, Ralph Taylor and John Roebuck.

Stuart Currie, Chairman of the Elsecar and Cortonwood Group and, behind, David Airey who succeeded David Bullock as Secretary.

Postscript

This book is being published as a tribute to Alan Hall in memory of his boundless energy and enthusiasm displayed whilst promoting the 'Barnsley Canals' and campaigning for their restoration.

Originally, Alan and I were to have produced *Forgotten Waterways of Yorkshire* as a joint effort using his superb collection of related photographs. Alas, this was not to be. In the early planning stages of the book, Alan suffered a fatal heart attack and any thoughts of publication were shelved for some time. However, Marie (Alan's widow) and Richard (his son) generously gave me the photograph collection, along with their blessing, to publish them in the format that Alan had discussed.

Alan's knowledge of the two canals was legendary, mine sketchy in comparison, and I would have had great difficulty in captioning many of the pictures without the much appreciated help of John Parry, a fellow Canal Group member.

Roger Glister

When editing the *Aspects of Barnsley* books my first port of call when searching for suitable canal illustrations and information was a visit to see Alan Hall. He was always kind and generous, loaning me material and providing 'off the cuff' facts and anecdotes, trawled from his many years of interest in the canals of Barnsley. Alan was a special guest when we launched what turned out to be the first (of seven) Aspects volumes.

We would often talk about producing a book on the Barnsley Canal, based on his considerable archive of photographs. Later, we would even swap medical information as we were both experiencing 'heart problems'. Eventually, when I began working as a commissioning editor for Wharncliffe Books, I had no hesitation in contacting Alan and we agreed, with the help of his friend and fellow canal enthusiast Roger Glister, to produce a 'definitive' but popular volume which would also include the Dearne & Dove. Understandably, Alan's

sudden death put the project 'on hold' until Roger agreed to continue as sole author, with the support of Marie and the Hall family. The book serves as a fitting tribute to Alan Hall but I can imagine Alan would have said that the book was, principally, for anyone interested in Barnsley's canals, their history and future restoration.

Brian Elliott